letters from the wild

volume 2

Jessica Matthews

E. E.

"Success is largely
not giving in,
long after others
have given up."

- My Great Aunty Val

Hey lovely,

I have these socks.

Black.

Short.

The kind that sit just under the ankle.

They have “L” and “R” printed on the toes.

Left.

Right.

Some mornings, without trying, I get it right.

Left on left. Right on right.

And when that happens, I feel strangely powerful.

Like things are aligned.

Like I could solve world peace before breakfast.

Other mornings, they're wrong.

Left on right. Right on left.

I notice.

I don't fix it.

There's something about walking around all day

knowing they're technically incorrect.

A quiet rebellion no one else can see.

On the "right" days, I feel steady.

Capable.

Almost holy.

On the “wrong” days, I feel mysterious.

Slightly dangerous.

Like an outlaw in activewear.

I like these socks.

They give me exactly what I need,

depending on the day.

Sending love,

Jessica

Hey lovely,

Sydney.

That's where she was moving.

Her husband had been offered an opportunity.

The kind people call amazing,

the kind you don't really get to weigh up properly.

It arrives already decided.

So they were going.

Rolling the dice.

Packing a life into boxes.

I hadn't seen her for just over a year.

Before that, we'd seen each other almost every day, our lives threaded together without effort.

Spontaneous coffee dates.

Friday night drinks after work.

Sticky dance floors mixed with headaches and brunches the next day.

The easy intimacy of being in the same space.

Now we were two hours apart on a map.

But emotionally we were already in different decades.

"*What an amazing opportunity*," I said.

"*What a great adventure for you both.*"

All true. All said properly.

All while something in me quietly folded in on itself.

I held her tight.

Longer than polite. Longer than necessary.

"*We'll absolutely keep in touch*," I said.

"*I'll fly up to see you.*"

As I said it, two silent tears arrived –

the kind that don't ask permission.

I knew, even as I spoke that this wasn't a promise I would keep in the way it deserved.

Not because I didn't care.

But because life has a way of filling the space before you realise it's gone.

Sydney had her now.

Her routines. Her mornings. Her becoming.

And what a lucky city it was.

Sending love,

Jessica

Hey lovely,

Red dress.

Pink skirt.

Orange top.

Blue jacket.

My wardrobe is a psychedelic kaleidoscope of colour.

Patterns.

Prints.

If it's loud, colourful, or a little chaotic, I want it.

I buy it.

I wear it.

I keep it.

There's a calm in it.

In choosing pieces that don't ask to be toned down.

In letting colour exist without needing to justify itself.

Ironically, it's when I stand out in a crowd that I feel the most settled.

A bright blue jacket against black and grey.

Clear edges.

No confusion about where or who I am.

I did try the black uniform once.

The polished look. The classic look.

The version that blends.

That's when I felt like a fraud.

That's when I felt conspicuous.

As if I'd put on someone else's clothes and forgotten how to carry myself.

Trying to look like the others was the moment I felt most exposed.

Pink never did that to me.

Or green.

Red never asked me to explain myself.

Colour didn't make me louder, it let me relax.

So I stay here.

With my red dresses.

My loud prints.

My not-quite-right skirts.

Not because they make me brave.

But because being myself, visibly and without disguise,

is where I can be.

Sending love,

Jessica

Hey lovely,

DO NOT EAT.

A small blue and white moisture-absorbing packet

sitting at the bottom of the tortillas.

Easy to miss.

Easy to discard.

It does its work quietly.

No grand flair.

No look-at-me moment.

Just there,

absorbing what would otherwise soften

everything,

holding the damp so the rest can stay intact.

I usually throw them straight in the bin.

Little regard.

Dinner to make.

Hands moving faster than my thoughts.

On to the next thing.

But tonight I didn't.

I picked it up.

Turned it over between my fingers.

Noticed how light it was.

And also how it wasn't.

That strange in-between weight of something
that's holding more than it shows.

I wondered what was actually inside.
What it's made of.
How it knows what to take on.
How it decides what stays with it and what's allowed to be spared.
How something so small can absorb so much of what's unwanted.
So much moisture. So much quiet spoilage.
And just keep it.

Without complaint. Without ceremony.
Without needing anyone to notice.

No one thanks the packet.
No one asks how full it's getting.
No one checks whether it's had enough.

It doesn't get eaten.

It doesn't get saved.

It just does the job it was made for,

right up until the moment it's no longer needed.

I stood there longer than necessary,

tortillas still sitting on the bench,

feeling the low, familiar ache of recognition.

How much holding happens like this.

Out of sight.

How often the work that protects everything else

can look like nothing at all to those

who don't see

the packet.

Sending love,

Jessica

Hey lovely,

I have these green heels.

Satin. Deep emerald.

Not sky-high, but high enough to change the way you stand.

The kind that lengthen your legs and remind you that posture is a choice.

I bought them when I was heavily pregnant.

2:17am.

Insomnia.

Wrestles legs.

I remember staring at them on my phone thinking - *yes*. These will definitely make me feel like a sexy woman again.

They lived in their box for 6 years.

Waiting.

Last night, I wore them.

An actual drink.

At night.

Without the kids or husband.

Just me and a friend.

I strutted from the car to the bar like it was a catwalk and I was the campaign face for "Women Who Still Have It."

My laugh was louder.

My hair flick was on point.

My shoulders back.

My glass swirling slowly in my hand like I owned 51% of the shares in the place.

People complimented them.

I smiled through the pinching.

Through the slow numbness in my toes.

Through the ache that crept up my calves.

I felt expensive.

Magnetic.

Unapologetic.

Like the woman I imagined I could be when I bought them at 2:17am all those years ago.

They hurt the whole night.

As soon as I got home, I put them straight into the donate pile before I even took my makeup off.

Sending love,

Jessica

Hey lovely,

A syringe filled with water.

Clear barrel.

Black measurement lines.

Exact amounts.

Push here, stop there, no guessing.

That's what they handed me when I was 15 doing work experience at a vet.

I had arrived with much bigger plans.

I was there to help animals.

Possibly assist in something important.

At the very least hold a clipboard with purpose.

Instead, I stood at a stainless steel sink pushing water in and out of a syringe so it would be "accurate."

Something about air bubbles.

Something about precision.

Push.

Release.

Check the line.

Push again.

It's funny what you notice when you're 15 and starting to realise something about yourself.

Because the syringe wasn't just precise,

it required you to *believe* in precision.

To trust that the right amount exists,

and that your job is to find it and stick to it.

I don't think I'd ever really lived that way.

I was never good at maths or science.

Or anything, really, that asked for a definite

answer before you were allowed to continue.

Anything that wanted a clean yes or no.

Black or white.

Up or down.

Correct or incorrect.

My brain just...

didn't live there.

And it still doesn't.

I live in grey.

In long conversations where the point isn't to win.

In ideas that don't need to land anywhere specific.

In feelings that don't always translate neatly into reasons.

I've always understood things more by sensing them than solving them.

Which, as it turns out, is not especially helpful in chemistry.

Or veterinary medicine.

They tend to want numbers.

And the right numbers.

Anyway. I live in grey.

Sending love,

Jessica

Hey lovely,

There's a "Keep Left" sign at the end of our road.

It sits on a tiny island where the single lane splits into two.

It keeps getting knocked down.

I'll drive past and it's bent sideways again.

Or flattened completely.

We report it. They fix it.

It stands up straight for a while.

Then someone hits it again.

And we repeat our reporting dance to the council.

I never see it happen.

I wonder who does it.

Are they distracted?

Speeding?

Just don't care?

It's such a small instruction.

Two words.

Keep

left.

And yet without it, you hesitate for a second at the roundabout.

Just long enough to feel unsure.

Sometimes I wonder what would happen if we didn't report it.

If we just left the sign there.

On the ground.

Sending love,

Jessica

Hey lovely,

An orange knit crop top.

And a matching orange knit skirt.

I found them in an op shop the other day, on one of those cold, grey afternoons where everything feels a bit dim and flat.

And there it was, this bright orange set, standing out against the darkness like it was already getting excited for summer.

Optimistic.

Slightly impatient.

Very sure of itself.

It stopped me immediately.

Because many years ago, I had a very committed crop-top phase.

Half my wardrobe was crops.

I wore them constantly.

To dinners.

To the supermarket.

To places where a crop top was arguably unnecessary but emotionally correct.

A boy I briefly dated once looked at me and said,

"Don't you own anything that's... long?"

I did not take this as feedback.

I loved them.

Still do, apparently, because I have a drawer in my cupboard dedicated to clothes from that era.

Not because I wear them.

Just because I'm not ready for them to not exist yet.

So when I saw this orange set, I was immediately in love.

It felt like something from a former version of me waving across time.

I bought it. Took it home.

Folded it carefully into the drawer.

And then recently, getting ready for a friend's birthday, I thought,
Alright. Let's see.

I put the crop on.

And it's not for me anymore.

Not in a sad way.
Just in a very straightforward, well-of-course kind of way.

No number of crunches, runs, or politely declining chocolate is going to change the fact that this stomach housed and birthed two nine-pound babies.

And I'm actually fine with that.

The skirt, though, looks fabulous.

Like amazingly fabulous.

Still bright.

Still confident.

Still entirely willing to be seen.

So the skirt is coming to the party.

The top can stay in the drawer a little longer.

Not gone.

Just...

resting.

Sending love,

Jessica

Hey lovely,

Six pink carnations.

Wrapped in cellophane.

A ribbon tied carefully at the front.

It really was a lovely thought.

A proper surprise.

The kind that arrives slightly awkwardly in someone's hand, already making the room feel softer.

"*You like them, don't you?*"

Of course I did.

Who doesn't like flowers.

Especially surprise flowers.

"*I knew carnations were your favourite.*"

And I paused.

Because they weren't.

I've always loved daisies.

Big, white, uncomplicatedly cheerful daisies.

I've said it for years. Never hidden it.

Briefly considered naming my daughter Daisy at one point.

Wear perfume called Daisy.

Even planted them in the garden, despite knowing full well I don't really have enough sun for them to thrive.

But in that moment, holding the carnations, I had this small,

strange wobble.

Maybe I do prefer carnations.

Maybe they're nicer.

Maybe they're more grown-up.

Maybe somehow they know me better than I know myself.

Maybe daisies were just a phase I accidentally committed to.

It only lasted a second or two.

That quiet little slip where you momentarily

outsource your own knowing.

Because the truth is,

I do think carnations are pretty.

And I do love surprise flowers.

Both of those things can be true.

But daisies are still my favourite.

Even if someone tells me otherwise.

Even if the carnations arrive wrapped in ribbon

and good intentions.

Even if, for a moment,

I almost believe it too.

Sending love,

Jessica

Hey lovely,

There are possums on our roof again.

I hear them most nights now.

Small feet scampering up and down.

The soft thud of a landing.

Our roof, apparently, a perfectly reasonable

highway between one tree and the next.

They're loudest just after the kids fall asleep, when the house finally settles into itself.

Lights off.

Dishes done or at least politely ignored.

No one asking for water or another story or the specific toy that cannot possibly wait until morning.

Most nights, I sit there in the dark.

Not lonely. Not sad.

Not even thinking very much.

Just sitting inside the quiet that nighttime makes possible.

I used to think silence meant something was missing. That it pointed to an emptiness.

A waiting.

A kind of unnamed longing that followed me from room to room.

But it doesn't feel like that anymore.

Now it feels warm.

Held, somehow.

Like the day has loosened its grip and nothing is being asked of me for a little while.

This is the time I feel most at peace.

When my shoulders drop without being told.

When ideas arrive gently, instead of needing to be chased.

I open my iPad and let the words come if they want to.

Slowly.

Unevenly.

Like rain deciding whether it's really going to start.

And above me, the possums keep going about

their business.

Back and forth across the roof.

Certain of where they're headed.

Unconcerned with whether anyone is listening.

The house is quiet.

The night is warm.

Nothing urgent is happening.

Sending love,

Jessica

Hey lovely,

A white ice cube tray.

Fourteen little rectangles.

Once upon a time it even had a lid, though that disappeared years ago and I've stopped expecting it back.

I never realised how much ice one house could possibly go through.

Even in the middle of winter.

Ice in water.

Ice in cordial.

Ice in juice.

Ice eaten straight from a spoon, apparently, like it's a perfectly normal snack and not something slightly feral.

Whenever I open the freezer, the tray is right there at the front.

Very visible. Very dependable.

And yet never full.

Even when I'm sure I filled it only a few days ago.

Even when I distinctly remember carrying it carefully to the freezer so it wouldn't slosh everywhere.

Even when I had that brief, satisfying thought of *there we go, sorted.*

Four or five cubes are always missing.

No one's taken them, of course.

Everyone denies it.

No one recalls using any ice recently.

No one even seems particularly interested in ice as a concept.

No one else even seems to notice them going missing.

And yet fourteen filled spots feels like this strangely elusive target.

I keep thinking this will be the week I manage it.

The week I open the freezer and there it is, completely full and triumphant.

It hasn't happened yet.

I refill it anyway.

Slide it back in.

Close the freezer with a small sense of optimism I probably haven't earned.

Sending love,

Jessica

Hey lovely,

Nan never used a chopping board.

She'd hold the apple in her hand,
blade sliding back and forth like it had always
known where to go.

I used to watch,

slightly horrified.

Certain she'd slice her thumb clean open.

She never did.

Slice after slice,

after slice.

Like she trusted her hands more than the rules.

She'd even be doing the crossword at the same time.

Apple in one hand.

Pen and knife together in the other.

Clue half-solved.

Knife moving without drama.

I don't even know if she really looked at what she was doing. She just knew.

I do it like that now.

No chopping board. No safety lecture.

Just the apple in my palm and the knife doing what it's done for decades.

There's something in that inheritance.

Not rebellion. Not recklessness.

Just a quiet belief that you can hold something sharp and not hurt yourself.

I liked that about her.

I like that about me.

Too.

Sending love,

Jessica

Hey lovely,

When we were dating, we used manual toothbrushes.

I kept a spare at his house.

He kept one at mine.

When I lived alone, his toothbrush would sit beside mine in the cup. They leaned into each other like they were hugging. Bristles touching. Handles tilted together.

Every morning while I washed my face, they'd be there,
pressed close,
like they'd spent the night whispering sweet nothings.
Like they were sharing secrets about us.
Like they knew things.

It was ridiculous and romantic all at once.
Two toothbrushes in love.

But now we use electric.
There are two handles. Two detachable heads.
Assigned colours. Assigned slots.

They don't lean.

They don't touch.

They stand upright in their charging docks, facing forward. Not even looking at each other.

Blue. Pink. His. Mine.

Efficient. Clinical. Quiet.

Sometimes I look at the space between them.

It reminds me of the time I cried to my Nan because I was certain Mum and Dad were going to get divorced.

She looked at me with warmth.

Reassurance.

And something else I didn't understand then.

And then she said, "No *they won't.*"

I didn't understand that look at the time.

I understand it now.

Some days I miss my old toothbrush.

But this electric one does a pretty good job.

Sending love,

Jessica

Hey lovely,

"Butt ends of the loaf."

Still gets a raucous laugh in our house.

It did when I was a kid too, if I think about it.

Some phrases have remarkable longevity.

The inside of the loaf is soft. Fluffy.

Vegemite rests on it like it's been given

somewhere nice to be.

No effort required. It just... holds.

But the butt ends...

Denser. Slightly curved.

The crust thicker, firmer.

Vegemite doesn't glide there. It catches.

You have to press a little harder with the knife.

It feels more deliberate.

More like a decision than a sandwich.

Neither girl likes the butt ends.

So their sandwiches are made with the clouds.

Not out of sacrifice.

Not even out of generosity.

Just necessity.

Someone has to eat them.

Which means, more often than not, my own sandwich is an impressive concentration of loaf ends.

Two pieces.

Stacked together like they volunteered.

I don't particularly like them either, for the record.

But they're fine.

Perfectly edible.

Still bread.

And there's something about standing at the bench, assembling lunches, knowing instinctively which pieces are mine without anyone saying it out loud.

No meeting.

No vote.

Just the quiet redistribution of softness.

Sending love,

Jessica

Hey lovely,

The left indicator goes on.

I hear it before I feel it.

Tick. Tick. Tick.

For a moment, I almost keep driving straight.

Not because anything is wrong.

Just because not turning would mean letting the day unfold without me checking in from a distance.

I know she has the best teachers.

I know she laughs a lot.

I know she is busy doing the important work of being small and growing, all at once.

She is absolutely fine.

Still, I turn left.

A quiet drive-by.

Not slowly enough to be noticed.

Not close enough to really see anything.

Just a soft loop past the place where she is spending her hours without me.

She won't see me.

And I won't see her.

But just because it's a day she's away from me

physically

doesn't mean it's a day she's away from me

emotionally.

There's something about that distance.

How ordinary it is.

How enormous it can feel anyway.

No emergency.

No problem to solve.

Just the small, steady stretch of loving someone

who is learning to belong to the world as well as

to you.

The indicator stops ticking eventually.

The road straightens.

The day keeps moving, like days do.

And somewhere, in a classroom I'm not part of,

she is busy being exactly who she is becoming.

I keep driving.

Sending love,

Jessica

Hey lovely,

The wardrobe door doesn't quite latch.

It hasn't since we moved in.

You can push it closed.

Line it up carefully.

Even hear the small click that says it's done what it's meant to do.

And then later,

it's open again.

Not wide.

Just enough.

A thin line of darkness where there shouldn't be one.

Maybe the house shifted.

Maybe the frame settled.

Maybe it was never hung properly to begin with.

I don't fix it.

When I walk past, I nudge it with my hip.

Push.

Click.

Carry on.

Some days it stays shut.

Other days it doesn't.

Some days we sit close without trying.

Other days we orbit each other,

efficient,

tired,

talking about logistics instead of anything heavier.

No drama.

No catastrophe.

Just something slightly misaligned.

The door is open again.

I press it closed.

Feel the resistance.

Wait for the click.

And leave it at that.

Sending love,

Jessica

Hey lovely,

There are yellow leaves already on our maple tree.

It sits in the middle of the backyard with its limbs stretched wide, like it's hugging the rest of the garden.

I've watched this tree change for years, and still, the first yellow leaves surprise me.

Not because I didn't know the season was coming.
Just because I wasn't expecting it yet.

Each year it feels sudden.
Even when it isn't.
I notice how quickly the colour appears.
How something that looked entirely green a
moment ago is already letting go in small ways.

Nothing dramatic.
Nothing urgent.
Just a shift you could almost miss
if you weren't looking straight at it.

I find myself standing there longer than
necessary,
as if the tree might explain something
it has never once tried to explain.

It just changes when it changes.

Without announcement.

Without checking if anyone else is ready.

Anyway.

Sending love,

Jessica

Hey lovely,

We have this new kettle.

It's stainless steel.

Sleek.

Slightly reflective in a way that makes you aware of your own face when you stand too close to it.

It feels like the kind of kettle adults buy once they've accepted they probably live here now.

Not a placeholder kettle.

Not a "this will do for now" kettle.

A commitment kettle.

Our first kettle was white and light.

You filled it.

Flicked a small lever, not even a button, and it boiled.

Then it stopped.

That was the entire relationship.

This one has options.

Seventy degrees.

Eighty. Ninety.

One hundred.

It assumes a level of tea knowledge I do not currently possess.

Apparently, water has nuance.

Apparently, there is a correct temperature for peppermint.

Apparently, chamomile has rules.

Apparently, adulthood involves knowing them.

I don't know what tea I have.

I just have tea.

Cupboard tea.

Emotional support tea.

Whatever was half price tea.

And now, instead of flicking a lever and moving on with my day, I stand there staring at numbers like I'm about to be assessed.

It shouldn't feel like a decision.

But somehow it does.

What if I'm overheating something delicate?

What if I'm ruining the subtle notes?

What if there aren't subtle notes?

I always press 100.

100 feels decisive. Confident. Unapologetic.

No one has ever criticised boiling water for being too hot.

This kettle also has a feature the product description was very excited about.

If it boils and you don't use it, it keeps the water warm. Simmering. Waiting.

And if you still don't use it, it beeps.

A polite reminder that your boiling water is ready whenever you are.

In theory, I liked this.

In practice...

I lay the teabag in the mug.

I should probably fold the washing while it boils.

I start matching socks. That blue one has been missing for weeks. I was just about to finish that thought about how maybe I...

Beep.

Right.

The kettle.

I walk back.

It's still hot.

Still waiting.

So am I, actually.

I was just about to pour the cup when...

"*Muuuuum?*"

Yes.

"*Where's the blue sock?*"

No idea. Try the couch.

Beep.

Right. Back to the bench. I pour the water.

Actually no...

I should wipe this spill first.

And the dishwasher needs emptying.

And while I'm here I'll just...

Beep.

It's reminding me.

As if I've forgotten.

As if I don't already have seventeen tabs open in my head.

As if I wouldn't prefer to be sitting with a cup of tea on the couch with my feet up.

Beep.

As if the problem is memory, not momentum.

Beep.

Alright already!

Eventually I do make the tea.

I drink it standing up.

It's lukewarm by the time I take my first sip.

Of course it is.

Sending love,

Jessica

Hey lovely,

I'm standing at the kitchen bench.

Not because I necessarily *want* to be.

But because this is where I feel most comfortable.

My legs are tired in that deep, humming way.
The kind that isn't bad enough to properly complain about,
but loud enough that you feel it behind your knees.

And now, the house is finally quiet.
Lunchboxes are washed.
School forms are submitted.
The dishwasher is doing that low, faithful hum it always does.

And instead of sitting,
instead of collapsing into the couch like a reasonable person,
I'm here.
Leaning on the edge of the bench.
Tea cooling beside me.
Writing.

It's funny how standing has become something I do.

My grandpa used to stand all the time.
We'd be at their place for dinner,
roast lamb, potatoes,
peas that rolled off your fork,
and there would always be enough chairs.

Plenty.

And yet he would stand.
Leaning forward at the bar.
Arms folded. Watching.

I used to wonder why he didn't just sit down.
Why he wouldn't pick a chair.
Why he stayed hovering on the edge of it all,
like he might leave at any moment.

Maybe sitting meant surrendering to the tiredness.

Maybe standing kept him alert.

Available.

Maybe it wasn't even that deep.

Maybe it was just habit.

And now here I am.

Leaning on a kitchen bench.

Writing a book I've squeezed into the margins of my own life.

My grandpa stood at the bar.

I stand at the bench.

Sending love,

Jessica

Hey lovely,

The bathroom scales sit beside the vanity.

Black.

Shiny.

Waiting.

I step on first.

Not because I need to.

Just because they're there.

There's that small, suspended second while the numbers blink.

Thinking.

Deciding.

And then they land.

Later, when I say I'm tired,

he says he's exhausted.

If I mention I didn't sleep well,

he says he was up too.

If I say I feel a bit flat,

he says his day was brutal.

It’s not a competition.

But sometimes it feels like one.

Like we’re both stepping onto invisible scales,

waiting to see whose number is higher.

Whose depletion counts more.

Whose weariness earns the first shower.

The first silence.

The right to not speak.

There’s no medal for winning this.

No prize for being the most undone.

And yet

some days it feels like we’re both quietly trying to

tip the balance.

I don’t even know when it started.

Maybe when survival became routine.

Maybe when we stopped asking how

each other were

and started reporting statistics instead.

Steps walked. Hours slept.

Meetings survived. Children managed.

Data.

Not tenderness.

The scales don't care.

I sometimes wonder what would happen

if neither of us stepped on.

If tired was just tired.

If hard was just hard.

If no one had to prove it.

The scales would still sit there.

Sending love,

Jessica

Hey lovely,

The dishwasher light is on.

Finished.

A small green glow in the dark kitchen.

Clean plates.

Clean cups.

Order restored.

There's something satisfying about it.

A task with edges.

A beginning.

A middle.

An end.

Finished.

Meanwhile, my night is still going.

Teeth not yet brushed.

One child calling out for water.

Another having an existential crisis.

There's a favourite teddy missing.

A school book not yet read.

A meltdown over the wrong set of pyjamas.

A sudden, urgent need to find a certain piece of paper that no one has mentioned all week.

There is no light that blinks when that's done.

No small green glow that says:

You may now rest.

The dishwasher hums.

Then clicks.

Then goes quiet.

I am still mid-cycle.

And sometimes I stand there in the kitchen,

looking at that light,

and think -

How lovely it must be to just finish.

Not dramatically.

Not resentfully.

Just factually.

Clean dishes stacked inside.

Night still open in my hands.

And no button to press.

Sending love,

Jessica

Hey lovely,

At kinder drop-off, there's a little iPad on the wall.

You tap the screen.

Enter your six-digit parent code.

Confirm the time.

Simple.

Most mornings I do it without thinking.

Shoes found.

Lunch packed.

Water bottle located.

Child delivered.

Tap.

Tap.

Done.

But every now and then, standing in front of that screen, my mind goes blank.

Six digits.

That's all it is.

Six digits I have entered hundreds of times.

And suddenly I don't know them.

I stand there staring at the screen while my daughter tugs at my sleeve.

"Mummmmmy."

I try again.

Wrong.

Again.

Wrong.

The teacher smiles kindly.

"It's *okay*."

But I can feel my face getting hot.

Not because the code matters.

But because I am already carrying so many things.

Permission slips.

Library days.

Who likes what snack.

When the birthday party starts.

Whether there are clean socks at home.

And sometimes it feels like all of it is balanced on a shelf inside my head.

Most days it stays there.

Some days a piece falls off.

A six-digit code.

A lunch order.

A clean uniform.

And for one brief moment I wonder if everything else might tumble down with it.

Eventually I remember.

I always do.

Tap.

Tap.

Confirm.

But I walk away thinking how the smallest failures can feel the biggest when you're already carrying so much.

Sending love,

Jessica

Hey lovely,

The lunchboxes are pink and red,

blue and yellow.

They have compartments.

Proper ones.

Little sealed sections for yoghurt so it doesn't leak into the biscuits.

A space for fruit.

A space for "sometimes food."

Even their own ice packs that slide into a hidden sleeve like they were designed by someone who has never had to panic-pack at 8:12am.

My red lunchbox was never this fancy.

It was hard plastic.

Clipped loudly.

One open cavity where everything lived together.

Sandwich, apple, biscuit if I was lucky.

No boundaries.

No compartments.

If the apple squished the sandwich, so be it.

I packed two lunchboxes, instead of the usual one, one Monday morning in February. First time ever.

Two sets of sandwiches.

Two drink bottles filled.

Two ice packs clicked into place.

Two little notes tucked into corners they might not even notice.

The pink-and-red one gets squares.

The blue-and-yellow one wants triangles.

No crusts here.

Crusts very much intact there.

I stood at the bench longer than necessary after I clipped them closed.

Two lunchboxes lined up side by side.

Balanced. Ready. Waiting to take on the world.

I remember when there was only one.

And before that,

none.

For years my job had edges.

Clear ones.

Baby at home.

Toddler at my hip.

Someone always needing something immediately.

Now, for two days a week, they both walk through

gates without me.

And I stand there holding empty hands.

The house doesn't echo.

It just...

settles.

I texted my mum that first week.

Verbatim:

"*I don't know what my job is anymore.*"

It felt dramatic even as I typed it.

But it wasn't about employment.

It was about usefulness.

About identity.

About who I am when no one needs their sandwich cut into shapes.

The lunchboxes sit on the bench until 8:43.

Then they're gone.

And for the first time,

so are they.

I rinse the knife.

Wipe down the crumbs.

And look at the two empty spaces where they were.

Two lunchboxes.

Two backpacks.

Two children stepping into the world without me beside them.

I didn't realise how much of me was packed into those little boxes too.

And how strange it would feel
to close the lid.

Sending love,

Jessica

Hey lovely,

There's a red bubble in the corner of my screen.

1,321 unread emails.

It used to shock me.

Now it just hums quietly.

Persistent.

Unblinking.

302 unread text messages.

Some days I don't even open them.

I read them in the notification preview instead.

Just enough to get the gist.

Just enough to know what's being asked.

Not enough to officially receive it.

Because once I open it,

it becomes real.

Once it's marked as read,

there's an invisible expectation attached.

So sometimes I leave it unopened.

Bold.

Waiting.

Other times, I open it.

Scan quickly.

And then swipe.

Marked as read.

Technically handled.

Emotionally untouched.

There's something about that swipe.

It clears the red bubble.

It makes it look like I'm on top of things.

But nothing has actually been answered.

I tell myself I'll reply later.

When I have the right words.

When I have energy.

When I can respond in a way that feels good enough.

Later comes. And I am tired.

And instead of replying,

instead of reducing what's on my plate,

I add something else.

A commitment.

A class.

A yes.

I've always been the kid in the front row.

Hand hovering.

Eager. Polite.

Wanting the teacher to nod.

Wanting to be seen as capable.

Helpful.

Good.

When I'm overwhelmed,

that part of me doesn't shrink.

She raises her hand higher.

Maybe if I keep saying yes,

I'll still belong.

Maybe if I stay useful,

no one will be disappointed.

Maybe if I don't open the message,

I don't have to risk answering it wrong.

I don't know.

All I know is the red bubble sits there.

And as I'm thinking about all of this,

another email arrives.

Subject line:

Naturopathy Certification – Enrol Now.

At 11:43 on a Tuesday night,

that feels like a version of me worth becoming.

Not because I want to study naturopathy.

But because it whispers:

you could.

You could be more.

You could be impressive.

You could be chosen.

I don't open it.

I let it sit there.

Bold.

And the number changes.

1,322.

Still growing.

Still waiting.

And somewhere in me,

that little girl in the front row

is still hoping someone will say,

"Good job."

Sending love,

Jessica

Hey lovely,

There's a group of magpies that live in the gum trees at the back of our yard.

Not just a pair.

A whole small committee.

You can tell when it's nesting season because the noise shifts.

Higher pitched.

More urgent.

Constant.

I used to assume it was just the mum doing the feeding.

That feels logical, familiar.

But if you stand still long enough, you see something else.

One digs.

One keeps watch.

One swoops low and then pulls back.

One lands on the fence and waits.

Another brings something small and wriggling in its beak.

They rotate.

Without discussion.

Without applause.

Without anyone announcing whose turn it is.

The chicks scream at dusk.

Open mouths.

Demanding.

Certain they will be fed.

And they are.

Not by one bird.

By whoever is closest.

Whoever has something.

Whoever is free enough in that moment to respond.

I've watched it a few times now.

The way they don't seem to count.

The way no one bird carries the whole evening.

I wonder what that feels like.

To land on a fence and know someone else has the next worm.

To fly off for a moment without calculating what's happening behind you.

To not be the only one who hears the urgency in the sound.

The magpies don't look heroic.

They don't look resentful.

They just move.

Village instinct.

Shared load.

No ceremony.

The light fades.

The chicks quiet.

The trees settle.

And I stand at the kitchen window for a second longer than necessary, watching them reorganise themselves for the night.

I wonder what that's like.

Sending love,

Jessica

Hey lovely,

My dad gave me a bonsai.

Not one he picked up on a whim.

Not one from Bunnings in a plastic pot.

One he had been growing for ten years.

Ten.

He handed it to me carefully.

Like something made of gold.

Like something that had already proven it could survive.

There were special scissors.

Tiny and precise.

And a book. Of course there was a book.

He told me how to water it.

How not to overwater it.

How to turn it slightly so it grows evenly.

How to prune without panicking.

I nodded.

Because that's what you do when someone gives you something they've nurtured for a decade.

You nod. You say thank you. You mean it.

But I didn't have the heart to tell him something else was also sitting in my chest.

It didn't feel like a gift.

It felt like an expectation.

Not a harsh one.
Not a cruel one.

Just another thing for me to keep alive.

Everything in my garden was chosen for ease.
Low maintenance.
Hardy.
Plants that forgive you if you forget them for a few days.
Or a few months.

The few that need regular maintenance,

well I chose them.

Which somehow makes the tending lighter.

This one was different.

Ten years of someone else's care.

Now handed over.

I spend too long standing in front of it.

Staring.

Trying to work out if the leaves look healthy.

If the soil is too dry.

If I'm already failing it.

The book sits on the bench.

If I have time to read a book,

it won't be about bonsais.

Not because I don't think they're beautiful.

They are.

But if I have time,

it will be for something that lets me exhale.

Not something that teaches me how not to get it wrong.

I worry about letting it down.

Which feels ridiculous, when I say it out loud.

It's a tree.

But it's not *just* a tree.

It's ten years of my dad's patience.

Ten years of clipping and shaping and believing something small can be guided into something remarkable.

And now it's in my hands.

Some days I look at it and feel proud.

Trusted.

Capable.

Other days I look at it and think –

I didn't ask to carry this.

Maybe it will thrive.

Maybe it won't.

Maybe loving something isn't the same as having the capacity to tend it perfectly.

I water it anyway.

Carefully.

Trying not to drown it.

Trying not to forget it.

Hoping that's enough.

Sending love,

Jessica

Hey lovely,

I once opened the front door wearing nothing but a green trench coat and a smile.

No warning.

No hesitation.

Just confidence and a hallway light behind me.

We were dating then.

The kind of dating where you'd call in sick to work
and stay in bed all day.
Where pub toilets felt rebellious.
Where there was always time.

I don't miss it.
That's the strange part.

He probably does.
I think he does.

Sometimes parcels arrive.
Small, hopeful things.
Folded lace.
Soft silk.
Boxes that sit unopened on my side of the wardrobe.

By the time I could wear them,

it's 9:17pm.

The dishwasher is blinking.

The house is quiet.

My body is done.

There is no green trench coat moment in me at that hour.

Only cotton pyjamas and relief.

And I don't feel sad.

I feel honest.

That season was real.

This one is too.

Some nights love looks like a hallway reveal.

Some nights it looks like sleep.

I close the wardrobe.

The boxes stay where they are.

Not rejected.

Just waiting for a woman who is not this tired.

Sending love,

Jessica

Hey lovely,

He’s talking to me.

I know he is.

I can see his mouth moving from the other end of the couch.

Something about tomorrow.

Or work.

Or a meeting.

Or someone he spoke to today.

I catch every third sentence.

The rest drift past me.

Not because I'm ignoring him.

Not because I don't care.

I do.

I really do.

But my brain feels like a browser with too many tabs open.

One child needs a costume by Friday.

The other needs a gold coin donation tomorrow.

Someone has outgrown their shoes.

Someone else has developed a sudden hatred of pasta after three years of eating nothing but pasta.

The washing is still in the machine.

There is probably a wet towel somewhere becoming a problem.

He's still talking.

I hear my name.

I look up.

Smile.

Nod.

Hope it was the right response.

For a moment I try to pull myself back into the conversation.

Really listen.

Really be there.

But another thought barges in.

Maybe I could just put the uniforms in the dryer?

And just like that, he's gone again.

Not physically.

Just somewhere beyond the static.

Eventually one of us stops trying.

I honestly couldn't tell you who.

Maybe he notices I'm somewhere else.

Maybe I realise I haven't heard a word he's said for fifteen minutes.

Maybe we're both too tired to rescue it.

The conversation dissolves between us.

No argument.

No slammed doors.

Just two exhausted people.

Eventually we head to bed,

content that the day has taken all it can from us.

The house is quiet.

The uniforms have been hung out.

Tomorrow will be here before we know it.

And just before I'm about to succumb to the night,

I hear "*muuuummmy*" calling from somewhere

down the hallway.

Sending love,

Jessica

Hey lovely,

There's a click in my left knee.

It happens on the back steps.

Third one down.

Click.

It's not painful.

Just audible.

When we lived in the inner city,

I wouldn't have heard it.

Trams.

Traffic.

Neighbours.

Life humming close by.

Out here, it's quiet.

Quiet enough to hear your own joints negotiating.

Click.

I love it here.

The trees. The space.

The possums on the roof.

But sometimes I miss the kind of noise that hides

you from yourself.

Now there's no hiding.

Just me.

My knee.

The third step.

Age isn't dramatic.

It's subtle.

It's cartilage clearing its throat.

Click.

And I laugh,

because I used to think grown-ups just arrived.

But I was wrong.

Turns out they click.

Sending love,

Jessica

Hey lovely,

Sometimes I think about my life as a backpack full of rocks.

Not all of them weigh the same.

Some are pebbles.

A load of washing.

A permission slip that needs to be submitted.

Realising we're out of toothpaste.

They make a small sound when they land.

Manageable.

Almost forgettable.

But then there are the bigger ones.

The questions.

Am I doing enough for the kids?

Did I listen properly today?

Did I miss something important while I was busy keeping everything moving?

Those don't slip quietly into the bag.

They land with weight.
A thud.

And then there are the rocks that aren't even mine.

The ones my daughters hand me when their feelings get too big.

Their anger.
Their tears.
Their nerves before something new.
The fears they don't yet know how to hold.

When a day collapses into a tantrum on the kitchen floor,
I sit with them and absorb it.

And sometimes it's the middle of the night.

A voice calling from the dark.

A bad dream that feels real enough to make their whole body shake.

I pull them close.

Tell them it's okay.

Let them fall back asleep.

They settle.

But the feeling doesn't disappear.

It has to go somewhere.

So I carry it.

Those are the heaviest rocks of all.

Because once their crying stops,

once their breathing slows,

once they run back to Lego or colouring or asking

what's for dessert,

they're lighter again.

But the feelings haven't vanished.

They've just moved.

Into my backpack.

Some days I'm good at emptying it.

I set the bag down somewhere in the afternoon.

Let the rocks spill across the floor.

Start again lighter.

Other days I don't realise how heavy it's become

until bedtime.

Until I'm brushing my teeth
and my shoulders ache a little.
Until I lie down and notice how tired my whole
body feels from carrying it upright all day.

Some nights I can fall asleep easily enough,
but the backpack is still there,
sitting quietly beside the bed,
waiting for morning.

And tomorrow,
like always,
I'll pick it up again.

Because some of the rocks are mine.

And some of them belong to the small people who
still need somewhere safe to leave them.

I'll carry their rocks until they have their own bag.

And maybe even then,

too.

Sending love,

Jessica

Hey lovely,

I lay my pink yoga mat at the front of the room.

Fold it out one way.

Then the other, so it doesn't curl back in on itself.

It's muscle memory now.

Through years of arriving early.

Lighting the candles.

Greeting each woman as she steps in, half-apologetic, half-hopeful.

Twenty women today.

More than I usually like.

I always say yes to one more.

There's always one more who "really needs it."

And I remember what that feels like to need somewhere to land.

So I make space.

I started these classes because I needed something.

Something that was mine.

A reason to leave the house.

A way to remember who I was underneath the logistics and the noise and the nappies.

I didn't say that out loud at the time.

I framed it as service.

As community. As a calling.

As holding space.

And I did hold it.

For years I held women's breathing.

Their pauses.

Their unraveling.

Their tears that slipped out during savasana.

Holding space is a privilege.

An honour.

But it takes something, too.

And somewhere between the pink mat and the

dim lights and the steady inhale-exhale rhythm,

I found what I came for.

I found myself.

Not in a lightning bolt way.

Not in a dramatic reinvention.

Just slowly. Quietly.

I stopped searching.

Today, as I smooth the corners of the mat flat

against the floorboards,

I *know* this is my last class.

Not because I'm burnt out. Not because I resent it.

Not because I can't hold anymore.

But because I don't need it in the same way.

I didn't start this to build an empire.

I started it to build myself back.

And I did.

The women will come in soon.

They'll unroll their mats.

They'll settle into their familiar spots.

I will guide them through the breath one more time.

And when I roll my mat up at the end,

I won't rush.

I'll do it gently.

With pride. With love. With respect.

Just like the mat,

I don’t want to curl in on myself either.

So maybe this isn’t an ending.

Maybe it’s just the moment you realise

you don’t need the structure that saved you

anymore.

Maybe it was never meant to be forever.

Maybe it just needed to be long enough.

And maybe that is enough.

Sending love,

Jessica

Hey lovely,

There's a white and red roller on the floor in our bedroom.

It's lying in front of the mirror where I left it earlier, after trying to roll out the tight muscle in my leg.

I had meant to put it away earlier, but I guess my day got away from me.

Mum called fifteen minutes before dinner.

Dad has another lump.

They're waiting to hear back from his oncologist.

That's all I know.

I'd already ordered takeaway because I didn't have the energy to cook.

The containers spread across the table.

Guacamole going brown at the edges.

I called them to the table. Passed the napkins.

Opened the sour cream.

Then I walked down the hallway and into the bedroom.

I didn't mean to cry.

I just needed a minute.

That's when I saw the roller.

It's such a simple thing.

You sit still.

You find the tight place.

You roll until it loosens.

I stood there staring at it, my eyes glazed over,

trying to keep the sound of my breathing steady

so they wouldn't hear.

The girls were laughing at something.

Cheese stretching from tortilla to plate.

The roller was still on the floor.

I wish fear worked like a muscle.

And I wish the roller was enough.

Sending love,

Jessica

Thank you for spending time with these quiet moments.

If you'd like to find more like this, you can visit:

www.wildwomanpress.com.au

Jessica Matthews
Wild Woman Press